STEWART ISLAND
RAKIURA NATIONAL PARK

Neville Peat

Otago University Press

Published by Otago University Press
Level 1, 398 Cumberland Street
Dunedin, New Zealand
university.press@otago.ac.nz
www.otago.ac.nz/press

First published 2000
Revised editions published 2015 and 2019
Copyright © Neville Peat
The moral rights of the author have been asserted.
ISBN 978-1-98-853170-0

Publisher: Rachel Scott
Editor: Jane Connor
Design/layout: Jane Connor
Maps: Allan J. Kynaston
Index: Imogen Coxhead

Front cover: Paterson Inlet. NEVILLE PEAT
Back cover: South Island saddleback on Ulva Island. MATT JONES

Printed in China through Asia Pacific Offset Ltd

CONTENTS

ACKNOWLEDGEMENTS

The author and publishers are grateful to Sharon Pasco, Diana Morris, Jon Spraggan and Kevin Carter for their assistance in revising this edition. Thanks also to the following residents for their advice and information for previous editions: Dale Chittenden, Brent Beaven, Ulva Goodwillie, Elaine and Bill Hamilton, Margaret and Colin Hopkins, Bruce Ford, Raymond Hector, Phillip Smith, Colleen Dawson, Peter Tait, Furhana Ahmed, Phred Dobbins, Noel Pasco, Dave Brownlie, Vicki Coats, Sharon and Pete Ross, Matt Jones, Jo Ricksen, Margaret Rooney and the late Ted Rooney.

All photographs are by the author unless otherwise acknowledged. For the use of photographs, many thanks to Dale Chittenden, Phred Dobbins, Lou Sanson, Greg Lind, Matt Jones, Sandra Whipp, Stephen Jaquiery, Brent Beaven, Rod Morris, Brian Patrick, the Department of Conservation and Rakiura Museum. Thanks also to Allan Kynaston for the maps.

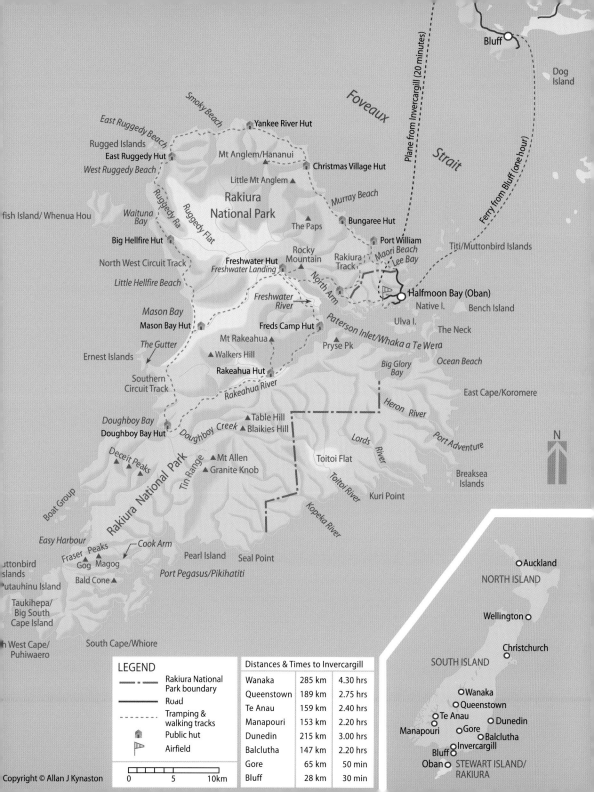

1

'TREASURE ISLAND'

STEWART ISLAND, known also as Rakiura, is a superlative place for many reasons. Of the three main islands of New Zealand, it is the smallest, southernmost and by far the most natural – a precious pendant on the South Island and separated from it by a shallow, moody stretch of water – Foveaux Strait. Settlement is confined to the northeast coast and centred on Halfmoon Bay, Horseshoe Bay and the township of Oban. It could be said that Stewart Island is what New Zealand looked like before cities and large towns came along – its natural heritage dominates, on land and in the surrounding sea.

Mostly unroaded wilderness, the island is a ragged triangle 75 km long by up to 45 km wide – similar in area to the Coromandel Peninsula. There are about 170 satellite islands and islets, the largest being 5 km-wide Codfish Island/Whenua Hou off the northwest coast, a cradle for early European–Maori settlement dating back to 1825 and today a nature reserve and last refuge for the critically endangered New Zealand parrot, kākāpō. Twenty small islands lie within Paterson Inlet/

LEFT: Boaties' paradise: yachts and motorboats at their moorings in sheltered Thule Bay in Paterson Inlet.
RIGHT: View from Observation Rock over Watercress Bay and Paterson Inlet.

Approaching the Ryans Creek airstrip near Halfmoon Bay. In the distance is Prices Point peninsula and Paterson Inlet.

Whaka a Te Wera, which forms a significant indent, about 100 sq km in extent, on the eastern coastline. The total coastline length of Stewart Island is 755 km.

Forested hills and ranges dominate the landscape. To the north of Paterson Inlet is the highest ground – the Anglem complex. At 980 m, Mt Anglem/Hananui is the island's high point. Towards the southern end of the island bare granite domes loom out of the landscape, marking a strange and harsh environment in which the forest becomes dwarfed.

Stewart Island is surrounded by vast tracts of the Southern Ocean on three sides. It spans latitudes 46 and 47°S – the 'Roaring Forties' latitudes, so named for their notoriously strong and persistent westerly winds. One of the world's great oceanic boundaries – the Subtropical Convergence – curves around the bottom of Stewart Island between it and The Snares, a subantarctic group of islands 100 km southwest. Water masses emanating from the Tasman Sea wash the Stewart Island coastline, moderating the climate of the island and protecting it from the cooler subantarctic surface water to the south of the convergence.

Visitors reach the island by air or sea. First impressions are of an island swathed in naturalness, with forest descending to the shoreline and overhanging secluded beaches of

GETTING THERE

Catamaran ferries and light aircraft cross Foveaux Strait daily. It is possible to mix the two forms of travel – fly one way, ferry the other.

The ferry service, operated by the 100-passenger *Foveaux Express* or the 60-passenger *Southern Express*, has scheduled morning and afternoon sailings from Bluff, which is about 20 minutes' drive south from Invercargill. The ferry company offers a shuttle service between Invercargill and Bluff. There are summer and winter timetables and the crossing takes an hour. The Halfmoon Bay wharf is a short walk from the centre of Oban township. Besides passengers, the ferries carry light freight, including kayaks; cars are transported to and from the island on a small freighter.

The air service operates from Invercargill Airport. There are at least three flights a day in both directions, with more flights as required, especially in the summer months. The planes, typically 10-seater twin-engined aircraft, use an airfield on a cleared ridgetop 2 km from the township and about 150 m above it. A minibus transfers passengers to and from Oban. There are weight limits on luggage.

Foveaux Strait ferry arriving at the Halfmoon Bay terminal.

creamy golden sand. Unlike the mainland areas north of Foveaux Strait, there are no expanses of pasture here, no widespread farming or recent forest clearance, and no roads beyond the village areas.

The island's economy is based on the sea and a steady stream of visitors. Commercial fishing boats target mainly crayfish (rock lobster), blue cod and pāua (abalone), although the number of vessels based at the island has fallen in recent years. Since the early 1980s salmon and mussel farms located in an arm of Paterson Inlet have provided jobs and an economic boost for the island. Crayfish destined for the international market are kept live in holding tanks then shipped out, chilled in bins, to Christchurch for export.

Tourism is the other major economic activity for the island and it accounts for a good number of the full-time jobs. Stewart Island receives about 40,000 visitors a year. Most are day visitors but increasing numbers come to experience the Rakiura Track, one of New Zealand's Great Walks, or spend several days exploring the bays and walkways in and around the settled

LEFT: Visitors to Ulva Island enjoy lunch among giant rimu trees. ABOVE: Fishing and recreational boats moored at Halfmoon Bay in silver sunshine.

area. Rakiura National Park, New Zealand's southernmost national park, is a strong drawcard. Groups of deer hunters, anglers and divers help swell visitor numbers, and visitors keen on tramping in remote areas can tackle the island's longer trekking circuits. Deer hunters (who require permits) have a network of relatively new huts available to them thanks to a project by the Rakiura Hunter Camp Trust.

Formed roads, just 25 km of them, are found only in and around the township area, serving an estimated 600 vehicles on the island. In contrast to the limited road network are the 245 km of walking tracks available across the island. In 2013 the local authority (Southland District Council) imposed a $5 levy (collected on ferry and air fares) on non-resident visitors to offset the cost of maintaining infrastructure, footpaths, local walking tracks, picnic tables and other amenities.

Cruise ships pay visits in spring and summer months, up to 20 of them in a season. Some bring more than 1500 passengers, for a few hours trebling the local population.

There is a mystique about Stewart Island that is not found elsewhere in New Zealand. It has to do with its wilderness atmosphere, haven qualities, limited development, small population and location off the beaten track. Pioneer botanist Leonard Cockayne wrote of Stewart Island

in the early 1900s: 'It is hard to speak of the scenery of Stewart Island without using a superabundance of superlatives.' Little has changed across the greater part of the island since Cockayne's day, and superlatives are still appropriate. Rakiura remains the most intact and natural – the least logged and built upon – of our three main islands.

It is a natural treasure – a green gem in a blue setting.

LEFT: Ulva Island forest. RIGHT: West End Beach, Ulva Island.

RAKIURA NATIONAL PARK

Rakiura is New Zealand's newest national park, covering about 85 per cent of the island, 157,000 hectares. The remainder includes buffer areas around the township and a large block of Māori land on the east coast from Paterson Inlet to south of Lords River. Codfish Island/Whenua Hou is excluded, as are the Māori-owned Tītī Islands, but the islands of Paterson Inlet, notably Ulva Island, form part of the national park.

Only land managed by the Department of Conservation was considered for national park status. The park was created following a public consultation process through 1998 and a recommendation from the New Zealand Conservation Authority in April 2000. Minister of Conservation Chris Carter formally approved the gazetting of Rakiura National Park in 2001 and it was opened on 9 March 2002 by the then prime minister, Helen Clark. At the time there was some concern that increased visitor numbers arising from national park status would spoil the village lifestyle and overload infrastructure such as sewerage, electricity services and roading. This has not happened, although the Southland District Council and Stewart Island Community Board, the local authorities responsible for the utilities, aim for continuous improvement.

National parks are created to protect distinctive scenery, fauna and flora. Recreational enjoyment of the country's natural heritage is another aim of national parks, so long as the recreation is compatible with nature preservation.

New Zealand was among the first countries to establish national parks. The origins go back to 1887, when the Māori chief Te Heuheu Tukino gifted the summits of the central North Island volcanoes to form the basis of Tongariro National Park. There are now four national parks in the North Island, nine in the South Island and one on Stewart Island. They comprise 2.9 million hectares, or just over 10 per cent of New Zealand's total land area.

MORE THAN ONE NAME

Rakiura is the 'twin' name for Stewart Island; the Māori and English names are officially recognised as interchangeable. Several other geographical features also carry interchangeable names, for example Mt Anglem/Hananui. Rakiura is the pre-eminent Māori name for the island, translated as 'The Island of Glowing Skies' – a reference not only to the lingering sunsets but also to the night-time displays of Aurora Australis, the Southern Lights. Rakiura is an abbreviation of Te Rakiura a Te Rakitamau, referring to the blushing embarrassment of a young man, Te Rakitamau, when he was refused the hand in marriage of both daughters of a chief of the island.

Rakiura has had at least two other Māori names. Te Puka a te Waka a Maui, 'The Anchor of Maui's Canoe', refers to the tradition of Maui's discovery of New Zealand and his use of the South Island as a canoe or platform from which he fished up the North Island. Stewart Island was the anchor (puka in the southern dialect; punga in the north) for his canoe. It was also known in early times as Motunui ('Large Island').

The island takes its European name from William Stewart, first officer of a sealing vessel,

the *Pegasus*, which in 1809 sailed into the southern harbour that now bears its name. Stewart made a detailed chart of Port Pegasus and subsequently produced a chart of the whole island that was published in 1816 in the *Oriental Navigator*. The editor called the island 'Stewart's Island' – the first printed reference to the name.

Stewart Island anchors more than Maui's canoe. It anchors in its rocks, rivers and rugged shores, and in its garnishment of plants and animals, the hope of generations unborn that places like this will always exist.

(Neville Peat, *Stewart Island: The last refuge,* 1992)

FIRST FOOTPRINTS

People first stepped ashore here about 700 years ago, according to archaeological evidence. They were early Māori. With their arrival, Rakiura became the southernmost settled land in all of Polynesia. They came in canoes and set up camps at many points along the coastline, marked today by midden, burial and canoe-landing sites.

As the island was too far south for kūmara (sweet potato) to flourish, these first settlers depended on fish from the sea, shellfish, seals, marine and forest birds, eels from the rivers

LEFT: A display of Aurora Australis/Southern Lights from Observation Rock. SANDRA WHIPP
ABOVE: Maui's mythical anchor chain, linking Stewart Island/Rakiura to the South Island, emerges at Lee Bay.

and the seasonal migrations of juvenile native fish (including whitebait species) into the rivers. They also utilised plant resources, including fruits and the rhizomes of the native bracken fern (*Pteridium esculentum*) from forest and bush.

Tītī (muttonbirds), the young of the sooty shearwater, became a staple food, gathered from Rakiura's huge colonies of these migratory birds. Preserved in kelp bags wrapped in the bark of tōtara (*Podocarpus totara*), tītī were also a major item of trade with people to the north. They remain a traditional harvest for Rakiura Māori through the months of April and May, the bulk of the harvest occurring on the Tītī Islands in Foveaux Strait and off the southwest coast of the main island.

Rakiura Māori had contact with Europeans about as early as Māori anywhere in New Zealand because sealing activities from the late 1700s and the whaling of the early 1800s had a southern focus. The Foveaux Strait area was much exploited by these early European expeditions. Intermarriage was widespread, with whalers marrying local women and settling after the shore whaling stations were abandoned.

Captain James Cook sailed past Rakiura in March 1770 without confirming it was an island. He charted the southern tip of the island as South Cape, linking the island with dotted lines

LEFT: An inviting bay on the Horseshoe Point track. ABOVE: South Cape, the southern tip of Stewart Island/ Rakiura. It was named by James Cook in 1770 as HMS *Endeavour* rounded what he thought was the bottom of mainland New Zealand.

to the South Island. More than 30 years elapsed following Cook's visits before charts showed Rakiura was indeed an island.

In 1804 the American sealer Owen Folger Smith sailed through the strait, which became known as Smith's Strait for a few years before the present name was applied in honour of Governor Foveaux of New South Wales.

WEATHER REPORT

Bathed by ocean currents originating in the South Tasman Sea, Stewart Island enjoys a cool-temperate climate that is typically 'oceanic' and not given to extremes. The weather here is generally milder than that of many southern South Island regions, with snow rarely lying at sea level in the winter months.

ABOVE: Flooded track between Mason Bay and Freshwater River. DALE CHITTENDEN   RIGHT: Horseshoe Bay, with Halfmoon Bay adjacent and the entrance to Paterson Inlet in the distance. SANDRA WHIPP

But conditions are not uniform across the island. The inhabited bays in the northeast enjoy distinctly sunnier and drier conditions than the land to the south and west, which are the first areas to receive the moist westerly airstreams radiating out of the Southern Ocean. Halfmoon Bay records about 1600 mm of rain a year (similar to that of the Bay of Plenty lowlands in the North Island) compared to annual readings of up to 5000 mm in the south. The rainfall is fairly evenly spread throughout the year. Rain days are high at 210 a year, but much of the rain comes in the form of showers or drizzle patches separated by fine breaks. Temperatures are moderate. At Halfmoon Bay in summer, the mean daily maximum is 16.6°C; in winter it is 9.9°C.

Westerly winds predominate, as suggested by the sweep of sand dunes exposed to the west and the shorn pattern of trees and shrubs. Gales from the southwest and northwest quarters are not uncommon. Snow may lie in patches on the tops of the Anglem mountains through late winter and spring.

It's worth following a weather forecaster's advice to visitors: pack a raincoat and warm clothing but don't be surprised if you encounter warm fine weather, especially along the northeast coast.

LIE OF THE LAND

Rakiura is the elevated tip of a granite 'iceberg'. There are geological links with the granite landmasses of Fiordland to the northwest and The Snares to the southeast. The bulk of the island intruded in semi-molten form into the original crust eons ago.

The southern granites are typically coarse-grained and speckled. The curiously stark granite domes encountered in the south have been exposed by physical weathering, including frost action and wind erosion, and by chemical weathering, a process known as exfoliation which involves the peeling off of layers of rock. This process prevents or delays soil development and the establishment of plant life.

Other rock types on the island include 300 million-year-old diorite and gabbro in the Anglem mountains and, to the south in the Pegasus area, quartzite and various kinds of schist up to about 400 million years old. Tin and tungsten mineralisation occurs on the crest of the Tin Range – the target of a short-lived tin-mining venture in the late 1880s.

The Rugged Islands off Rakiura's rarely visited northwest corner.

A depression filled by Paterson Inlet and the Freshwater valley divides the island into two blocks, which would have been separate islands when sea levels were lower during the ice ages. The Anglem massif and Ruggedy Mountains dominate the northern block, which represents about a fifth of the total land area. The Ruggedy Mountains rise steeply from the coastline to reach a height of over 500 m within 1 km of the sea. To the south are Mt Rakeahua (681 m), Table Hill (716 m) and the Tin Range's Mt Allen, highest of the southern mountains at 750 m. In the bleak and hilly far south of the island, there is a subantarctic feel to the terrain.

Throughout, the island is well watered. Most streams and rivers flow eastward as a result of relatively recent geological uplift and tilting. The island's largest rivers – Freshwater and Rakeahua – rise in the western mountains. These two rivers were once tributaries of a larger river that flowed the length of Paterson Inlet when sea levels were lower. That larger river's mouth lay well east of the present coastline. Paterson Inlet was created when, about 10,000 years ago, the last of the ice ages gave way to a warming climate and rising sea levels. Around that time, the land bridges with the South Island were flooded to create Foveaux Strait, which is fairly shallow, with depths in the order of 20–40 m on the ferry route. At its narrowest, the strait is 27 km wide.

Stewart Island is also known for its swamps and bogs. Freshwater Valley contains the most extensive wetlands.

TOP: Bald Cone (230 m) is prominent on the western shore of South Arm, Port Pegasus. GREG LIND
BOTTOM: Bellhopper Falls, in the northernmost cove of Port Pegasus, is a little-visited scenic feature.

GETTING AROUND

Transport is reasonably easy to access in Halfmoon Bay. If you want to stay in and around the township areas, you can hire a car, scooter, electric bike or mountain bike, remembering of course that there are only about 30 km of formed roads. There is also a choice of guided tours on land or by boat.

Swift water taxis offer sightseeing trips, especially to Ulva Island and the marine farms in Paterson Inlet. Larger vessels specialise in guided scenic, fishing or diving trips. Charters for bird-watching, deer-hunting, fishing and historic places sightseeing are also available.

The advent of water taxis has allowed visitors relatively quick access to sections of the Rakiura Track that take several hours to walk. You can turn a day walk there and back into a shorter boat–walk experience by, for example, taking a water taxi to Port William on the northeast coast or North Arm in Paterson Inlet and walking back to the township areas. Water taxis and launches are often used by deer hunters for drop-offs in remote locations. Some parties arrive directly from Bluff or other ports in their own or chartered vessels and bypass Halfmoon Bay.

Sea kayaking around the eastern bays and harbours and in Paterson Inlet has become popular in recent years. Half-day or full-day guided trips in Paterson Inlet are popular with inexperienced kayakers.

Water taxi *Henerata* negotiating Freshwater River on a shuttle to Freshwater Hut. RAKIURA CHARTERS

2

TOWN AND AROUND

A FISHING VILLAGE with a solid stake in tourism, the Stewart Island settlement centred on Halfmoon Bay is a breath of fresh air – a place of enchanting walks and scenic surprises. Oban is the township at the heart of the settlement, which spreads across the hills and beaches to Horseshoe Bay on the northern side and to Golden Bay, Thule Bay and Ringaringa Beach on the southern, or Paterson Inlet, side. Homes and holiday cottages peep out of the bush, with a couple of church spires the only skyline development. Halfmoon Bay is a green amphitheatre that faces the sheltered waters of the bay and turns its back on the prevailing westerly winds.

Resonating with birdsong, Oban is a showcase town for native birdlife, thanks to concerted efforts to control predators. Melodious tūī and bellbirds (makomako) are conspicuous and active all day, and there is a large population of the playful and vocal forest parrot, kākā.

European settlement began in Halfmoon Bay in the 1860s. The township was not surveyed until 1877, and it soon became a fishing and sawmilling base. Although the timber-milling era ended decades ago, commercial fishing of coast and strait has endured and continues to evolve, with processing plants at both Halfmoon Bay and Horseshoe Bay handling blue cod and paua, and holding tanks for live crayfish.

The Oban Presbyterian Church commands a view over Halfmoon Bay.

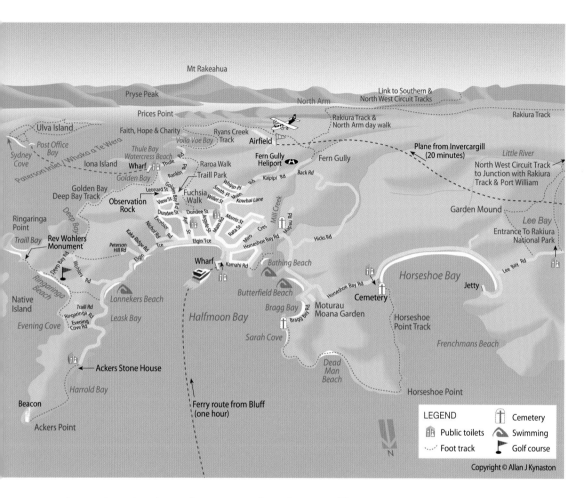

Map Legend:
LEGEND
🚻 Public toilets
⚐ Foot track
♱ Cemetery
⛰ Swimming
⛳ Golf course

N

Copyright © Allan J Kynaston

Aquaculture involves salmon, mussels and oysters. The island has a resident population of close to 400. Most jobs are either in commercial fishing, fish-farming and processing, or in the visitor industry.

Tourism is nothing new to the island, but today's visitors encounter more services and facilities than ever before. Opportunities abound in outdoor recreation – walking, long-distance tramping, golfing, fishing, diving, kayaking, sailing, sightseeing, deer-hunting and bird-

NAMES SWITCHED

Halfmoon Bay is misnamed. The HMS *Acheron* survey of 1857 switched the names for Halfmoon and Horseshoe bays, which were first mapped in 1844.

watching. There are a number of cafés in the town. Internet access took a leap forward in 2014 with the installation of new Wi-Fi technology and mobile phones now operate consistently across most of the residential area.

The $5-per-head levy for visitors earned $85,000 in the first year, 2013. It continues to fund developments for tourists, including new or upgraded footpaths, picnic tables and seats, and improvements in local walking tracks. The opening of Rakiura National Park has helped Stewart Island sell itself to international visitors, including backpackers and those seeking upmarket accommodation.

Township infrastructure made a giant leap forward in 1988, when a diesel power plant began delivering reticulated electricity; before then, residents relied on their own household generators. The cost to consumers is high compared to mainland charges. Investigations into alternative renewable power sources are ongoing.

Oban's infrastructure took another stride in 1998 when a town sewage scheme was commissioned with capacity for development in the future. Domestic water supply, though, is still largely based on tanks collecting roof water.

To the locals, Invercargill and the South Island are collectively known as 'The Other Side' or more simply, 'Town'. Although a police officer is based on the island, crime is rare.

In September 1999 a $2 million community centre was opened, incor-

The Golden Bay jetty with Iona Island behind.

porating a gymnasium and basketball court, function rooms, kitchen and library – a huge effort in community fundraising and self-help. Timber for the centre, including matai boards for the flooring, was shipped in from 'The Other Side'.

In recent years the rise of stylish lodges – through refurbishment or new construction – has been a feature of the tourist accommodation on the island. Visitors now have an extensive choice of more than 40 places to stay. Options include bed and breakfast, homestays, motels, lodges, holiday homes, cottages, apartments, cabins, backpacker hostels and a hotel. The historic South Sea Hotel, by the waterfront at Oban, is the only hotel on the island. Private campsites with washing and cooking facilities are also available in the township.

VISITOR INFORMATION

The Stewart Island Promotion Association maintains a website containing comprehensive visitor information: www.stewartisland.co.nz.

A free map of the township and a free wi-fi service in Ayr Street are funded from the Stewart Island visitor levy. Maps and other information are available from most business outlets.

TOP: Alfresco chess on the Oban waterfront opposite the South Sea Hotel. BOTTOM: Locals – a miniature horse entertains its master outside a café.

THINGS TO DO

Rakiura Museum: Many of the island's historic heirlooms reside at the local museum opposite the Community Centre in Ayr Street. From October to May (spring, summer and autumn), it is open Monday to Saturday from 10 am to 1.30 pm, and on Sunday from noon to 2 pm. When cruise ships are visiting the museum is open for longer hours. Through the winter months (June to September) it is open only around the middle of the day. The island's early Māori life, whaling, timber-milling and natural history are all featured. Among the more interesting artefacts are a dolphin-tooth necklace, nineteenth-century scrimshaw, and a revolver that was owned by the island's first magistrate. A new purpose-built museum is due to open in 2020.

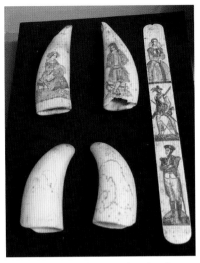

Rakiura Museum features the island's maritime history, including this whale-teeth scrimshaw artwork.

Shopping: The general store on the waterfront – besides offering a range of food, groceries and general merchandise (anything from a needle to an anchor, they say) – is a good place to see locals come and go. There is a boutique merino shop (Glowing Sky) adjacent to the general store, and books and gifts are available from two outlets on Main Road: Stewart Island Gift Shop and Rakiura National Park Visitor Centre.

Kiwi spotting: On Stewart Island kiwi far outnumber the residents. Stewart Island's tokoeka, a species of brown kiwi, live in the vicinity of the township, thanks to a commuity-led predator trapping programme. Various options are available for kiwi spotting around the Halfmoon Bay area and beyond to Ocean Beach and

A Stewart Island kiwi or tokoeka probing for sand hoppers on Ocean Beach.
MATT JONES

Mason Bay. Trampers using the Mason Bay Hut often hear kiwi calling at night, and the birds are sometimes seen foraging in the dunes or tussock grassland during daylight hours.

Golfing: On a forested island with little open space, a golf course is somewhat unexpected. The six-hole Ringaringa Heights golf course, a 30-minute walk from downtown Oban, offers panoramic views across the entrance to Paterson Inlet and neighbouring islands, including Native Island and Ringaringa Passage. Golf clubs can be hired at the post office.

The six-hole Ringaringa Heights golf course near Halfmoon Bay is a surprising recreational asset for an island with so much forest and shrubland. Native Island is beyond the narrow passage into Paterson Inlet.

SHORT WALKS

Stewart Island is a walker's paradise – even walking the sealed roads around town can be a scenic experience. But watch out for local cars. There are few footpaths beyond the flat waterfront area of Oban.

The Rakiura National Park Visitor Centre has detailed information on the local walks. Here are the highlights. For the tracks that start further out, consider taking a shuttle, or hiring a car, scooter or mountain bike to reduce the walking on roads. There are increasing opportunities for mountain-biking; check out bike access west of Oban in the direction of Kaipipi.

Distances from Oban waterfront:

Observation Rock – 0.5 km

Thule Bay – 1 km

Evening Cove – 3 km

Moturau Moana Garden – 2 km

Lee Bay – 5 km

Golden Bay – 0.75 km

Deep Bay – 2 km

Ackers Point – 4 km

Horseshoe Bay – 3 km

Fuchsia Walk

This bush walk is the closest to the township centre and the shortest. Take the road to Golden Bay and look out for the start of the track near the first intersection (Dundee Street). Uphill from here, this delightful walk takes about 5 minutes and emerges at Traill Park near Golden Bay Road. The walk is named for the native tree fuchsia (kōtukutuku, *Fuchsia excorticata*), which is recognisable by its pale-orange, papery, peeling bark and, in summer, its purple-green flowers with blue pollen. The fruit (kōnini) is a delicious dark-purple drupe, favourite food of bellbirds and kererū (New Zealand pigeon). Flocks of kākā (a forest parrot) are often found here.

Observation Rock

Stewart Island's most-visited lookout, Observation Rock is a 15-minute walk from the waterfront. Access is off Golden Bay Road. The panorama on a clear day takes in the Anglem mountains in the distance to the right, Mt Rakeahua and a large tract of Paterson Inlet. Ulva Island is to the left, and Golden Bay and Thule are in the foreground. Sunsets are especially glowing and impressive from here, reflected on the water. The small patch of bush surrounding the lookout is popular with native birds, including kākāriki (parakeets), bellbirds and tūī. Watch out after dark for displays of Aurora Australis/Southern Lights.

TOP: The tree fuchsia, *Fuchsia excorticata*, the world's largest fuchsia, is abundant on Stewart Island and immediately identifiable by its pale-orange papery bark. BOTTOM: A road sign at Traill Park warns motorists to watch out for kiwi crossing at night.

Raroa

Less steep but 15 minutes longer than the Fuchsia Walk, this 800 m track starts at Traill Park (on the opposite side to where Fuchsia Walk emerges) and winds down through fern-rich rimu forest to Watercress Beach at Thule. Some of the rimu (*Dacrydium cupressinum*) trees here would have been growing before humans set foot on the island about 800 years ago. The track is often alive with bush birds such as tūī, bellbirds, grey warbler (riroriro) and fantail (pīwakawaka). Return by way of the road or the walkway. From downtown Oban to Watercress via Fuchsia and Raroa walks takes about 40 minutes.

Ringaringa Point/Deep Bay, Golden Bay

Allow up to 2 hours for this circuit over roads and tracks – an introduction to elements of the natural history and human history of the island. The destination, Ringaringa Point, is a lonely headland overlooking Native Island and a channel linking Paterson Inlet with the open sea. Going clockwise around the circuit, head out from downtown Oban to picturesque Lonnekers Beach, then take Wohlers Road and Deep Bay Road, passing the golf course along the way. At the end of Deep Bay Road is eroding Ringaringa Beach, from where the track to Wohlers monument is signposted. The Rev. J.F.H. Wohlers was a pioneer missionary who served the Foveaux Strait area for 40 years in the mid-1800s. The monument to Wohlers and his wife is on the high ground overlooking the sea. A few minutes further on, below a slope of silver tussock, is the final resting place of the Rev. Wohlers, his wife and members of his family. The picket-fence graveyard is under a grove of big, old, weather-beaten macrocarpa (Monterey cypress) trees. Beside the macrocarpas is a large specimen of the native tree daisy tētēaweka

LEFT: Raroa walkway – a showcase of ferns. RIGHT: The graveyard of the pioneering Wohlers and Traill families is surrounded by a picket fence under massive wind-shorn macrocarpa trees.

(*Olearia oporina*), which bears spectacular flowers in spring. For the walk back, detour off Deep Bay Road to follow a bush track around the shoreline to Golden Bay. There are plenty of steps up and down. The glimpses of Paterson Inlet add to the experience.

Ackers Point

The bush-clad southern headland of Halfmoon Bay, Ackers Point features a beacon and colonies of tītī and little blue penguins (kororā). There is a road two-thirds of the way out to the point, passing Lonnekers Beach and Leask Bay. At Harrold Bay, shortly after the start of the walkway, there is an historic stone house, the oldest building still standing on the island. It was erected in the 1830s by Lewis Acker, who arrived during the whaling era. In 1860, Captain James Harrold moved into the bay. He built a new house and used Acker's cottage as a smithy and later as a boat-building workshop; visitors can see some old tools inside. There is a beacon at Ackers Point, about 15 minutes walk further on. Replaced by a new unit several years ago, the original beacon was installed at Ackers Point in 1927 to mark the

Ackers Cottage at Harrold Bay. Lewis Acker built boats here from the 1830s, as did Captain James Harrold in the 1860s. RAKIURA MUSEUM

entrance to Halfmoon Bay. There are views ahead to the Tītī/Muttonbird Islands, with flat-topped Bench Island – a nature reserve – out to the right. Tītī and penguins have burrows in the bush surrounding the beacon. Visitors must remain on the formed track. The tītī return to their burrows at dusk during the summer/early autumn breeding season; the little blue penguins – smallest of all penguins – are often active at night. Visitors are asked not to disturb them. Allow 3 hours for the walk to Ackers Point and return. Note that access to Harrold Bay is courtesy of the landowners.

ABOVE: The oldest building on the island is the stone cottage built by whaler Lewis Acker at Harrold Bay in the 1830s.
BELOW: A mature rimu tree surrounded by a carpet of moss.

Horseshoe Point

Another impressive lookout about 50 m above sea level, Horseshoe Point can be accessed from a 3.5 km coastal loop track off Horseshoe Bay Road at Moturau Moana Garden or further on where Horseshoe Bay Road meets the bay. The walk takes about an hour one way from Moturau, or 30 minutes from the Horsehoe Bay access point 3 km from downtown Oban. The latter track is one of the flattest and easiest of the local walkways, and the views from the trig point are rewarding, especially as the headland is not forested. Large old exotic macrocarpas and bluegums line sections of the track, hinting at more habitation than exists here today. On a clear day look out for The Neck away to the south, Bench Island and the Tītī Islands, the closest of which are Herekopare and Jacky Lee. If there is a breeze, Buller's mollymawks and perhaps other albatross species will be patrolling the ocean in front of the point. Fishing vessels processing their catch on the way back to port attract these large sea birds.

The walk along Horseshoe Bay Road offers many varied views of bays and beaches, with Bathing Beach the first one encountered. Short tracks to the beach lead off Kamahi Road. Just past Butterfield Beach is Moturau Moana Garden, where a maze of paths leads visitors through grassed compartments surrounded by native trees, shrubs and ferns. Some of the trees here, common north of Foveaux Strait, are not found naturally on the island, including beeches and various other flowering trees: kōwhai, karo (*Pittosporum crassifolium*) and tarata (lemonwood, *P. eugenioides*). There is a lookout here over Halfmoon Bay. Moturau Moana was gifted to the government and the people of Stewart Island by the late Noeline Baker.

Garden Mound

Mature and complex forest of podocarps (a family of mostly Southern Hemisphere conifers), studded with large rimu trees, is a

Southern rātā flowering beside the native grass tree *Dracophyllum longifolium*. The rātā flowers appear in December–January.

feature of this walk, which involves a climb to about 160 m above sea level. Access is off the Lee Bay Road beyond Horseshoe Bay. An opening in the forest near the summit affords views towards Horseshoe and Halfmoon bays. There is an opportunity to do a circuit taking in the Garden Mound summit, Little River and Lee Bay.

Little River

The Lee Bay–Little River leg, just over 1 km long, forms part of the Rakiura Track. It sidles the coastal hills through tall forest before dropping down to Little River's intimate and charming estuary, where rātā and other trees overhang the tidal and silt flats. At low tide, it is possible to walk a distance up the edge of the river.

This short walk gives visitors a taste of Stewart Island forest and seashore – essential elements of the island's character.

ULVA ISLAND

A superb place for family bush walks and a flagship for conservation, Ulva Island in Paterson Inlet is a short water-taxi ride from Golden Bay or (longer) from Halfmoon Bay. Visitors usually land at the jetty at Post Office Bay, where a sign points out natural and historic features. The cottages here are on a patch of private land, although the 267 hectare island is essentially one big reserve and an open sanctuary for threatened wildlife. There is a picnic area, shelter and toilet at Sydney Cove beach, 5 minutes walk from the jetty.

Beyond Post Office Bay and Sydney Cove – where giant pine, macrocarpa and southern beech trees were planted by the Traill brothers, Charles and Walter, in the late 1800s – the forest is old-growth indigenous and contains many ancient rimu and tōtara trees.

Historic Post Office Bay, Ulva Island. The cottages and boatshed are privately owned.

Ulva was set aside as a reserve in 1899, an early date for conservation efforts. It has become a sanctuary for the South Island kākā, and two kākāriki (red-crowned and yellow-crowned parakeets). Weka, cheeky flightless native woodhens, are usually conspicuous around Post Office Bay, where they will approach visitors in search of treats. They may even try to snatch your sandwich! All birdlife on Ulva has benefited from the eradication of rats in 1997. The absence of predators has allowed endangered birds such as the yellowhead (mohua) and South Island saddleback (tīeke) to be reintroduced. The first transfer of saddlebacks from sanctuary islands off the west coast of Rakiura was carried out in April 2000. Because the reintroduction of rats would be disastrous for the birds, vessels tying up at Ulva are requested to check for rats on board.

Ulva, about 4 km long, is the largest island in Paterson Inlet and lies across the seaward end of the inlet, where two marine reserves (1075 hectares in extent) are located to protect marine life. The western end of the island offers the easiest walking. The tracks at the hilly eastern end are steeper and less well maintained.

Post Office Bay marks the site of Stewart Island's first post office (1872–94). It was established here by Charles Traill because Ulva was midway between the European settlements at The Neck and Halfmoon Bay. The Department of Conservation maintains the island's tracks and facilities with the support of the Ulva Island Charitable Trust, a community group.

FISHING CONSTRAINTS

Paterson Inlet is a popular place for recreational anglers, but rules apply to sustain the fishery. Commercial fishers have agreed not to harvest from the inlet, and charter-boat operators are asked to abide by a code of practice. Catches are restricted, and visiting fishers should be aware of the latest fishing regulations. There are daily limits for blue cod and crayfish. Trading of any fish species is forbidden. A marine reserve straddles Ulva Island – a no-take area that spans Paterson Inlet on either side of Ulva .

3

TRAMPING

THE ONLY WAY TO FULLY EXPERIENCE Stewart Island is to set out on foot for days on end, pack on back and equipped for any sort of weather – in other words, go tramping, which is the New Zealand term for back-country trekking or hiking.

There are three main tramping circuits – the Rakiura Track, the North West Circuit and the Southern Circuit. The Southern Circuit overlaps with the North West Circuit on the Mason Bay–Freshwater Landing section.

Because of the strenuous going, muddy sections of track and the likelihood of rain or cold snaps occurring at some time on the longer circuits, trampers are advised to take plenty of food, a portable stove and warm clothing. As a Department of Conservation notice at the Rakiura National Park Visitor Centre warns: 'All seasons can be experienced in a day.' Strong footwear is recommended. In places, long sections of boardwalk have been built over soft, wet sections of track to avoid damage to vulnerable vegetation.

For safety's sake, check out weather and track conditions at the national park visitor

Track flood warning on the track between Freshwater River and Mason Bay. DALE CHITTENDEN

HAZARDS: MUD AND BITING FLIES

Stewart Island's longer circuits are notorious for their muddy sections, which are the product of saturated, poorly drained, acidic soils and a wet climate. Some sections are slow going because of the mud.

Biting blackflies, better known as sandflies, are a pervasive nuisance, hence the warning to carry insect repellant to protect exposed skin. They are rife on Stewart Island in lowland forest as well as on open beaches. Only two of the 13 native species bite, and only the adult females of these two species bite (to obtain protein for egg-laying); but they are common enough to be a widespread nuisance. The itchy feeling is caused by the anticoagulant pumped into the victim by the fly to prevent sucked blood from clogging the insect's proboscis. As well as humans, they target birds, bats, seals and lizards.

centre at Halfmoon Bay before setting out on the longer tramps, and remember that your safety is your responsibility. You can let a friend or family member know of your intentions through the website Adventure Smart New Zealand (www.adventuresmart.org.nz). It is also a good idea to take a personal locator beacon, which can be hired.

RAKIURA TRACK · 32 km

The Rakiura Track is Stewart Island's premier tramping experience. It can be comfortably walked in three days, from either direction and at any time of year. The round trip anti-clockwise out of Halfmoon Bay involves three legs (8, 13, 11 km long) with huts at Port William on the northeast coast and North Arm on the Paterson Inlet

LEFT: Climbing to a high point on the Rakiura Track near Port William. ABOVE: Port William beach, shaded by gum trees.

side. Both huts have 24 bunks and bookings are necessary to stay at the huts and campsites. Fees are charged per person, per night. For more details, visit the Department of Conservation website (www.doc.govt.nz/ … rakiura-track).

As one of New Zealand's Great Walks, the Rakiura Track ranks in status with the likes of the Abel Tasman, Milford and Routeburn tracks. A Great Walks hut pass can be purchased online or from the Rakiura National Park Visitor Centre at Halfmoon Bay (or from DOC's Invercargill office) before trampers set out. There is no charge for day use of the track.

The huts have mattresses, stoves for heating, running water and toilets. The Rakiura Track is one of the shorter and easier Great Walks tracks, and it has the advantage of being a circuit. The Port William–North Arm leg crosses hill country up to 200 m above sea level. In recent years, the long stretches of boardwalk constructed in the 1990s have been replaced by a hardened, more natural surface, and above Port William the track has been rerouted to take in a historical site featuring old log haulers.

The total distance from Halfmoon Bay is 39 km, which includes 5 km of road to Lee Bay and 2 km of road linking with the North Arm (Kaipipi) leg. Trampers often take a shuttle to the start of the track at Lee Bay.

Besides giving an introduction to Stewart Island's forest, sea-shore and bird life, the Rakiura Track is a lesson on the island's human history. Port William, or Potirepo, was an early Māori settlement site. From the early 1800s it harboured European sealers and whalers. In the 1860s a small amount of gold was found on the beach but a gold rush never eventuated. Port William's eucalyptus (gum) trees are remnants of a failed settlement by Scottish Shetland islanders in the 1870s. The area was later utilised by sawmillers, whose relics include a rusting boiler at the southern end of Maori Beach.

On the North Arm side there is evidence of early sawmilling (Sawdust Bay) and whaling (Prices Inlet).

NORTH WEST CIRCUIT · 125 km

A challenging tramp of 9 to 11 days for fit, well-equipped and experienced hikers, the North West Circuit skirts the northern shores of Stewart Island and links through to the Paterson Inlet shoreline via the Freshwater and Mason Bay flats. It is one of New Zealand's longest designated tramps. The beginning and final sections of the circuit utilise separate legs of the Rakiura Track. With the start/finish at Halfmoon Bay, the circuit is 125 km long. This includes 7 km of road linking Halfmoon Bay with the Lee Bay and North Arm (Kaipipi) track ends.

The swing bridge over Maori Creek at the western end of Maori Beach.

Although it roughly follows the coast for most of the way, the track touches beaches at only a few spots. These include Maori Beach (Port William), Bungaree, Murray Beach (between Bungaree and Christmas Village huts), Smoky Beach (near the most northerly part of the circuit), and East Ruggedy Beach, Little Hellfire Beach and Mason Bay on the western side of the island. Mud may be

RIGHT: Sawmill relics at Maori Beach, including a boiler. BELOW: Bungaree Hut on the North West Circuit.

Mt Anglem/Hananui, with patches of snow on the 980 m summit, rises above a small lake that was carved long ago by glacier ice. The track from Christmas Village Hut follows the lip of the lake.

encountered in some forested areas that have not had boardwalk installed. All huts have 12 bunks except for Bungaree (16), Yankee River (16) Mason Bay (20), and the two on the Rakiura Track – Port William and North Arm, which have space for 24 trampers. There are 10 huts on the circuit and the legs between them range from 6 km (Port William–Bungaree) to 15 km (Big Hellfire–Mason Bay).

Side trips at various places along the way will extend the tramping time by a couple of days. On the east coast, many trampers pause at Christmas Village Hut for a day to visit the summit of Mt Anglem/Hananui (980 m), the island's highest peak. This side trip, 11 km return, takes about 6 hours but can be very muddy. It illustrates a striking sequence of vegetation types, from lush coastal forest through dense shrubland to open subalpine meadow, herbfield and cushionfield near the summit. In spring and summer many of the alpine plants are in flower, including the spectacular great mountain buttercup (*Ranunculus lyallii*), whose white flowers are an emblem of Aoraki/Mt Cook. Christmas Village, incidentally, is not a village at all; it offers only a trampers' hut and a separate six-bunk hunters' hut.

Further down the coast at Mason Bay, trampers may choose to spend a day walking from the Mason Bay Hut near the middle of the bay to the southern end of the beach and back, a total

distance of about 14 km. The bay's southern end has The Gutter, an interesting area. From Mason Bay anticlockwise, the North West Circuit passes through tussocky flat land that was formerly a sheep farm (the historic homestead is a highlight) in the direction of Freshwater Landing, and Freshwater and North Arm huts on the Rakiura Track. This section has low-lying areas that are prone to flooding. From Freshwater Hut, a 3-hour-return side trip offers access to the summit of Rocky Mountain (549 m; a less well-maintained track), from where there are good views over the Freshwater flats and Paterson Inlet.

Despite the challenges of weather and mud, trampers on the North West Circuit generally return well rewarded – and certainly a lot fitter. Up to about 1000 trampers tackle this route every year, compared to about 2500 a year using the Freshwater–Mason Bay track.

SOUTHERN CIRCUIT · 74 km

The Southern Circuit, another challenging and remote tramp, loops from Mason Bay to Freshwater River. Not as well used as the North West Circuit, the Southern Circuit offers trampers a more compact experience of the wilds of Stewart Island, with more coverage of inland areas,

TOP: Ruggedy Mountains on the North West Circuit.
ABOVE: The historic Island Hill homestead, 1.7 km from Mason Bay beach.

Doughboy Creek and beach on the Southern Circuit.

notably the Rakeahua valley. A few fit and adventurous trampers combine both circuits – a grand-slam experience.

Just as mud- and weather-prone, the Southern Circuit takes five or six days. A popular option is to take a boat to Freshwater Landing and Freshwater Hut (16 bunks) and start walking from there, in either direction. Going clockwise, the huts are Fred's Camp (10 bunks), Rakeahua (6 bunks), Doughboy Bay (8 bunks), and Mason Bay (20 bunks). The longest leg is between the Doughboy Bay and Mason Bay huts – 18 km, which takes about 7 hours.

For more information about the North West Circuit and Southern Circuit tramps, visit the Department of Conservation website www.doc.govt.nz/ … rakiura.

MASON BAY

Mason Bay, Stewart Island's longest beach, is a highlight of the North West and Southern circuits. A 14 km-long arc of sand, bounded by Mason Head at the northern end and the Ernest Islands in the south, the bay is exposed to the prevailing westerly winds, which have built up an impressive set of sand dunes behind the beach. Especially well developed immediately north and south of Mason Bay Hut, the dunes extend inland for 3 km and climb to 150 m above sea level.

Amid the duneland there is an unearthly atmosphere, created in part by extensive stonefields, outlandish rock outcrops and strange sand patterns. Aeolian (from Aeolus, the Greek god of wind) is how geologists describe the dunes, which have excited wild and poetic thoughts down the years. A naturalist and gentleman farmer from Hawkes Bay, Herbert Guthrie-Smith, after a visit in 1911, described Mason Bay thus: 'Westward lies an alien continent across vast water solitudes, eastward dry dunes, the playground of the wind. Blown sand, clear skies, heaven's vault above, and space illimitable, these are the features of the bay.'

The duneland ecosystem is of special interest to biologists. It supports a suite of threatened, rare and localised plants, including one of New Zealand's rarest species, the small mat-forming herb *Gunnera hamiltonii*. The Mason Bay dunes are a showcase area for the orange native

The Ernest Islands at the southern end of Mason Bay are hammered by a westerly gale.

sandbinder pīngao (*Ficinia spiralis*), which has been displaced in many parts of New Zealand by introduced marram grass but which here, thanks to intervention from the Department of Conservation, is holding its own against the invasive marram.

Inland, the Mason Bay flats spread east to the foothills of the forested Mt Rakeahua. The flats contain 14 sq km of tussock grassland, featuring the tall and magnificent copper tussock. This is kiwi country. The island's tokoeka may be seen foraging in daylight in the tussockland, duneland and forest margins.

Sheep farming, which began here in the late 1870s, knocked back the tussock but it has recovered since the Island Hill farm was closed in 1987. The Mason Bay flats, together with the Freshwater flats, form the most extensive flat land on the island – a corridor for the sea as sea levels rise. In a direct line, Paterson Inlet is only 13 km from Mason Bay.

Light aircraft are able to land on the beach at mid- to low tide, and some trampers, kiwi-spotters and scientific groups seeking quick access to Mason Bay charter planes from Invercargill.

LEAVE NO TRACE

Minimise your environmental impact while you enjoy natural and cultural heritage areas. Guiding principles include: plan carefully, steer clear of fragile areas, dispose of waste responsibly, resist souveniring things, take care with fires, respect wildlife, be considerate of others.

Refer to the website www.doc.govt.nz/parks-and-recreation/ … leave-no-trace

4

A RARE AND SPECIAL NATURE

AS THE LEAST-MODIFIED of New Zealand's three main islands, Rakiura contains many natural features that are rare and special, which reinforced the case for creating a national park across the bulk of the island. Whereas large areas of the North and South islands of New Zealand have had their basic nature altered almost beyond recognition, the opposite is true of Rakiura, where the natural pattern remains substantially unmodified. Botanist Hugh Wilson describes the island as 'a natural wilderness, a remnant of old New Zealand, from wild coastline to scrub-barred tops'.

In a wider geographical context, the island has been likened to an 'ecological stepping stone' between the South Island mainland and the subantarctic zone. As a result of its strategic location, climate and topography, Rakiura is host to numerous plants, birds and animal species that are unique to it. It is also a showcase of uninterrupted vegetation sequences – from seashore to alpine summit. Coastal shrubland, coastal and lowland forest, duneland, wetland, grassland, subalpine shrubland, and alpine herbfield and cushionfield – one

Dense shrubland guards these granite domes and peaks in the wild south of Stewart Island.

ecosystem flows into another, depending on height above sea level, soil type and exposure to wind and sun, to form a seamless mosaic.

STEWART ISLAND'S PLANTS

Without beech species to define the treeline, as in the South Island ranges, the vegetation in upland areas develops a progressively lower stature until, in the alpine zone, it becomes tundra-like. More than half the land is covered by podocarp and hardwood (including southern rātā, *Metrosideros umbellata*) forest. Podocarp trees such as rimu (*Dacrydium cupressinum*), kahikatea (*Dacrycarpus dacrydioides*), tōtara (*Podocarpus totara*), matai (*Prumnopitys taxifolia*) and miro (*P. ferruginea*) are at their southern limit on Rakiura. They do not grow as tall here as in other parts of New Zealand, although rimu will reach a height of 25 m in northern parts of the island, where it dominates the forest canopy. Of the four smaller podocarp species occurring on the island, yellow-silver pine (*Lepidothamnus intermedius*) is widespread in

OPPOSITE, TOP: A tarn in the Tin Range area surrounded by low forest and granite domes. LOU SANSON. OPPOSITE, BOTTOM: Cook Arm, Port Pegasus, with the granite peaks of Gog and Magog in the distance. Islands in Cook Arm have retained forest cover but heath-like vegetation is typical of surrounding areas, where introduced deer roam and fire scars persist. TOP: Rimu forest on Garden Mound. LEFT: Mauve flowers of *Olearia avicenniifolia*, a tree daisy, at Mason Bay.

LEFT: Tētēaweka, the island's distinctive tree daisy *Olearia oporina*, produces spectacular flowers in spring; the flowers have either purple or yellow centres. This species of tree daisy grows near the coast and is found only at Rakiura and Fiordland. RIGHT: The wind-blown tops of the Tin Range support a mosaic of shrubs and grasses.

the south, reaching 9 m in height. Pygmy pine (*L. laxifolius*), pink pine (*Halocarpus biformis*) and bog pine (*H. bidwillii*) are also components of the low forest of the south.

Coastal shrubland features the island's well-known 'muttonbird scrub', which is a kind of tree daisy – the leathery-leaved puheretaiko (*Brachyglottis rotundifolia*). Also common on windswept coastal sites is another tree daisy, tētēaweka (*Olearia oporina*), which is restricted to Stewart Island and Fiordland, and a coastal form of leatherwood, *Brachyglottis colensoi*. Grass tree or inaka (*Dracophyllum longifolium*) and shore hebe (*Hebe elliptica*) are often associated with these tree daisies.

The duneland ecosystems, with Mason Bay the largest and Smoky Beach among the most intact, are special in a national context. No fewer than eight beaches on the island are ranked nationally important. Other ecosystems that are nationally important are the Freshwater Valley and Rakeahua wetlands and the Toi Toi flats.

But perhaps the most special habitat of all is the island's alpine zone, which has no fewer than 21 endemic plants, most being herbs or dwarf shrubs. Interestingly, seven occur only in the northern (Anglem) part of the island and seven are exclusively southern species, suggesting isolation of the two areas for long periods in the past. The remaining seven endemics are found in both the northern and southern blocks. There are endemic speargrasses (*Aciphylla* species), mountain daisies (*Celmisia*), buttercups (*Ranunculus*) and tussock grasses (*Chionochloa*). The complete absence of introduced plants is an outstanding feature of Rakiura's alpine zone.

Another feature of Rakiura plant life is the list of 'absentees' – species that are common north of Foveaux Strait but either missing altogether or extremely rare on the island, except where they have been planted by people around the settled areas. The missing species include the southern beeches (previously *Nothofagus*, now *Fuscospora* and *Lophozonia*), kaikawaka or New Zealand cedar (*Libocedrus bidwillii*), kōwhai (*Sophora* species), tarata or lemonwood (*Pittosporum eugenioides*) and māhoe (*Melicytus ramiflorus*). Kānuka (*Kunzea*) is also absent, although it is not found through much of Southland either. Cabbage trees (*Cordyline* species) are remarkably few in number, and the bulrush or raupō (*Typha angustifolia*), common north of Foveaux Strait, is entirely absent from Rakiura's wetland areas.

RIGHT, ABOVE: Dense muttonbird scrub, comprising one or more species of tree daisy, is common close to the sea in the company of southern rātā. This bush edge is at Boulder Beach, Ulva Island.
RIGHT: Rakiura's rarest plant is this creeping duneland herb, *Gunnera hamiltonii*, found only at Mason Bay, Doughboy Bay and West Ruggedy.

This list of 'lost species' has long puzzled botanists and biogeographers. The absence of beech is thought to be linked to the impacts of glaciation and/or cold climates during the ice ages. There are beech gaps elsewhere in New Zealand, notably through central Westland.

BIRDS

Rakiura is well known for its bird life, some of it quite special. Without Stewart Island, the critically endangered parrot kākāpō (*Strigops habroptilus*) would probably be extinct by now. Hopes for the recovery of kākāpō now depend largely on birds rescued from cat predation in the Pegasus area, where kākāpō were rediscovered in the 1970s. All known kākāpō have been removed from this area, the latest as recently as 1997, and predator-free Codfish Island/Whenua Hou is a stronghold now. In 2018 Whenua Hou held 67 kākāpō or 45 per cent of a world population of 149.

A kākāpō from Codfish Island/Whenua Hou. STEPHEN JAQUIERY

Much more abundant on the island are kiwi or tokoeka (*Apteryx australis*). Thousands survive on the main island, despite the wild cats, with a few living also on Ulva. Within the kiwi world, Rakiura's birds are the odd ones out in terms of their social patterns and the way they feed in daylight as well as at night. In other parts of New Zealand, young kiwi disperse within two or three weeks of hatching, whereas on Rakiura they are more likely to associate with their families for at least a couple of years. This may give them added protection from cats. As strange is the fact they are often seen feeding during the day, particularly in the tussock grassland and duneland areas of Mason Bay. It is thought this habit may be related to both the long daylight hours of summer and the difficulty tokoeka face of finding enough invertebrate food in the acidic soils during the short hours of darkness. Kiwi are found in forest, shrublands and dunelands across the main island, and even in and around the Halfmoon Bay and Horseshoe Bay residential areas.

A completely different bird – another Stewart Island star – is the southern New Zealand dotterel (*Charadrius obscurus obscurus*), a distinct subspecies; the only other dotterels of its kind live in the upper half of the North Island. Like the island's kiwi, it behaves differently from its northern cousins. Instead of breeding at the coast, as its northern counterparts do, it nests among dwarf shrubs and cushion plants on the mountain ranges, among them Table Hill, Tin Range, Mt Rakeahua and Rocky Mountain. In autumn the dotterels flock at coastal locations. They eat mainly insects, as does the commonest bird on the ranges, the New Zealand pipit (*Anthus novaeseelandiae*).

Forest birds are numerous. The most common are bellbird (makomako, *Anthornis melanura*), tūī (*Prosthemadera novaeseelandiae*), grey warbler (riroriro, *Gerygone igata*), South Island fantail (pīwakawaka, *Rhipidura fuliginosa fuliginosa*) and South Island tomtit (ngirungiru, *Petroica macrocephala macrocephala*). Bellbird and tūī are fiercely territorial and defend their territories and food resources – mostly berries and nectar – with strong melodious calls. The squeaking, jinking fantail, Stewart Island robin (kakaruai, *Petroica australis rakiura*) and quieter tomtit will

TOP: Rare bird: a male New Zealand dotterel in subalpine vegetation. DOC CENTRE: Bellbird feeding on the nectar of an introduced fuchsia species at Post Office Bay, Ulva Island. BOTTOM: Stewart Island robin and nestlings. BRENT BEAVEN

be attracted to people walking through the forest. These birds are hoping the visitor will accidentally provide a meal by disturbing insects in the foliage or on the forest floor. The last major population of Stewart Island robin survives on the Freshwater–Mason Bay flats and lowlands. Robins also live in good numbers on the island sanctuary of Ulva. The species is slightly smaller and darker than the South Island robin.

Weka are also likely to approach people. Inquisitive ground birds of the rail family, the Stewart Island weka (*Gallirallus australis scottii*) is a subspecies of – and smaller than – mainland weka. Beaches are good places to encounter these birds, and also the shrill-voiced variable (black) oystercatcher (*Haematopus unicolor*), whose chicks are often seen through summer – watch out for them on Maori Beach and at Port William. The Stewart Island fernbird (mātātā, *Bowdleria punctata stewartiana*), another subspecies, inhabits mainly shrubland in wet areas and across the tussock-covered flats.

The parrot family is well represented on Rakiura. Besides the kākāpō on Codfish Island/Whenua Hou, the main island

TOP: The Stewart Island weka or native woodhen, an endemic subspecies and the smallest of the various weka found throughout New Zealand, is a flightless rail that feeds mainly on invertebrate animals, fruit and seeds. CENTRE: A kākā framed by tree fern fronds. BOTTOM: Red-crowned parakeets or kākāriki are common on Rakiura and its outliers.

A healthy population of the endangered South Island saddleback inhabits Ulva Island. MATT JONES

supports a reasonable population of South Island kākā (*Nestor meridionalis*), a threatened species. Kākā are common around Halfmoon Bay and the settled areas. Around dusk and in the morning they may fly over the township singly or in noisy flocks. Their calls vary between liquid gurgling and harsh grating noises – often a surprise to visitors on Ulva Island. Rakiura is also a stronghold for two native parakeets or kākāriki – red-crowned (*Cyanoramphus novaeseelandiae*) and yellow-crowned (*C. auriceps*). In the South Island, yellow-crowned tend to outnumber red-crowned, but on Rakiura, the tables are turned and red-crowned are more common.

Rakiura, including its outliers, is definitely a last refuge for the South Island saddleback or tīeke (*Philesturnus carunculatus*). About the size of a blackbird but glossier, the saddleback belongs to a distinctive family of New Zealand wattlebirds. Fleshy orange wattles sprout from soft skin at the base of the bill, rather like they do on a domestic hen. Forming a saddle across its back is a band of bright chestnut feathers. Its relatives are the huia (*Heteralocha acutirostris*), which is now extinct, and kōkako (*Callaeas* species), the South Island species of which is on the brink of extinction.

The saddleback's Māori name, tīeke, gives a clue to its call – a repeated tee-eggy, tee-eggy, tee-eggy. The bird is a noisy forager that scratches vigorously in the leaf litter and tears at dead wood with its bill, thus advertising its presence to predators like rats and cats. The saddleback has been extinct on the main island since the early 1900s but it has survived on small predator-free islands off the west coast, thanks to a rescue operation in the 1960s by wildlife staff. Ulva Island offers visitors the best chance of seeing South Island saddlebacks.

Rakiura's most mysterious bird is the South Island kōkako or orange-wattled crow *Callaeas cinerea*. Botanist Leonard Cockayne reported good numbers south of Paterson Inlet in 1909, but it is now almost certainly extinct on the island. Expeditions go looking for kōkako from time to time but no traces of them have been found since the discovery in the Rakeahua valley in 1987 of feathers and moss grubbings characteristic of kōkako foraging.

Land birds are what most people think of in terms of Stewart Island wildlife conservation, but the island's rare and special fauna is not confined to birds. There are endemic species among lizards, freshwater fish and small invertebrate animals – as there are among the birds – and discoveries continue to be made, reflecting the remoteness of many habitats.

REPTILES

The lizard fauna is special. Among Rakiura's six known lizard species, three are unique to it. They include New Zealand's most spectacularly patterned gecko, the 12 cm-long Harlequin gecko (*Tukutuku rakiurae*), discovered in 1969 but not formally described until the 1980s. It lives mainly in dwarf shrubland and cushion vegetation on the Tin Range and other upland areas. A discovery of the early 1990s was the

Two lizard species found only on Stewart Island: the Harlequin gecko (top) and small-eared skink (bottom).
PHRED DOBBINS

small-eared skink *Oligosoma stenotis*, which lives in upland areas and on summit ridges on the Anglem massif and Tin Range. One of four skink species on the main island, it is brown and stripy on top, and green underneath. The three other skinks are southern skink (*O. notosaurus*), another endemic species, which is restricted to Rakiura and Codfish Island/ Whenua Hou, green skink (*O. chloronoton*) and common skink (*O. nigriplantare*). A second gecko species, the endemic *Hoplodactylus nebulosus*, is found only on Codfish Island/Whenua Hou and the Tītī Islands of the southwest.

BATS

New Zealand's two remaining species of bat – long-tailed (*Chalinolobus tuberculata*) and the nationally endangered lesser short-tailed (*Mystacina tuberculata*) – are both found here. They are curiously small bats, the short-tailed's body being little bigger than a mouse. Codfish Island/Whenua Hou is a stronghold for this rare species, which spends much of its time scurrying about like a mouse on the forest floor. Its long-tailed cousin is found in tall forest on the main island.

In 1998–99 there were sightings of an usual-looking bat on remote Putauhinu Island, off the southwest coast. Equipment that monitors bat echolocation calls suggested the island could be supporting a small population of the greater short-tailed bat (*M. robusta*), previously thought to be extinct.

INVERTEBRATES

Rakiura's invertebrate fauna, including the insects, is of special interest to entomologists, not so much for its diversity but for its endemic elements. Of 133 alpine insects identified in a survey in the early 1990s, 33 – or just on a

TOP: The nationally endangered lesser short-tailed bat (*Mystacina tuberculata*). ROD MORRIS
ABOVE: *Paranotoreas opipara* is one of 15 specialist geometrid moths found in alpine Stewart Island. BRIAN PATRICK

TOP: The chafer beetle *Prodontria praelatella* inhabits the dunelands at Mason Bay. BRIAN PATRICK

ABOVE: The giant kōkopu, *Galaxias argenteus*, which grows to over 40 cm in length, is widespread and common in the rivers, streams and swamps of Stewart Island, where no trout exist to compete with it. STEPHEN MOORE

quarter – are found only on Stewart Island. Beetles inhabit all ecosystems, from duneland to alpine cushionfield, and many are undescribed species. At least two are known to be unique to Rakiura, both flightless chafers – *Prodontria rakiurensis* from the Tin Range tussockland and *P. grandis*, a threatened species inhabiting short tussockland and herbfield, on Mt Anglem/Hananui.

FRESHWATER FISH

The island's freshwater communites are often overlooked for their value to biodiversity. Rakiura's aquatic and wetland life is about as pristine as you can find in New Zealand. From estuary to headwaters, habitats are unmodified and introduced species are virtually nonexistent. Streams and rivers appear to be entirely free of trout, which elsewhere in New Zealand have impacted adversely on the native fish.

Rakiura has 15 known native freshwater fish species, with more perhaps awaiting discovery. They include six galaxiids, scaleless fish whose ancestry traces back over 80 million years to the supercontinent of Gondwana.

In recent years a new galaxiid has been described – the small, swamp-dwelling *Galaxias gollumoides*. Long-finned (*Anguilla dieffenbachia*) and short-finned (*A. australis*) eel species and New Zealand lamprey (*Geotria australis*) are also found here, and the freshwater crayfish *Paranephrops zealandicus* is distributed widely. It has been found in streams at altitudes of 700 m.

ISLAND 'ARKS'

Two of Rakiura's 170 satellite islands and islets – Codfish Island/Whenua Hou and Ulva Island – are flag carriers for endangered species.

At 1359 hectares, Codfish Island/Whenua Hou is the largest and most important. Cliffed, hilly and forest-clad, it supports an astonishing complement of birds – some 65 species altogether. It is a veritable 'ark'. More kākāpō – in the order of 50 – live here than anywhere else. The island's Māori name means New Land, a hopeful name as this species is being pulled back from the brink of extinction.

Codfish Island/Whenua Hou is 3 km from the Ruggedy coast and out of swimming range of rats and deer, but before it could play a role in endangered-species work, it had to be cleared of weka and possums. Weka were brought over from the main island in the early 1800s by sealers as food, and possums were introduced for their fur. Both species were removed in the 1980s, weka because they were eating the eggs of the burrowing Cook's petrel (*Pterodroma cookii*), whose only colony in southern New Zealand is on this island. Possums, which can cause forest dieback if left unchecked, would have eaten kākāpō's food supplies and perhaps taken their priceless eggs.

In 1987 the first kākāpō were introduced to Codfish Island/Whenua Hou, which is now a nature reserve – the highest form of protection. Everyone requires a permit to land there; scientists, wildlife rangers and volunteers and descendants of the sealers and their Māori wives are among the few people who get ashore there.

Ulva Island (267 hectares) in Paterson Inlet is a different concept – a predator-free wildlife sanctuary, cleared of possums and rats, that is open to the public. Although South Island saddlebacks are its most precious species, visitors can also meet weka up close and enjoy glimpses of kākā, kākāriki and, occasionally, yellow-eyed penguins. There have been transfers of threatened yellowhead (mohua, *Mohoua ochrocephala*), a forest songbird of the South Island.

Other small predator-free islands close to Rakiura may become sanctuaries for endangered species in the future. They include Bench Island (121 hectares), off the Paterson Inlet entrance, which also has nature-reserve status and is free of deer, possums and rats. Its forest cover is in near-pristine condition – jungle-like, with ferns and understorey trees prolific. It has breeding populations of yellow-eyed and Fiordland crested penguins, Foveaux shag and New Zealand fur seal.

SEA BIRDS AND MARINE MAMMALS

Rakiura's marine life – as divers and anglers can testify – is hugely valuable and interesting. The main island and its many outliers constitute important breeding and resting sites for numerous sea birds and marine mammals.

More than 20 sea-bird species nest here. They include three penguin species – yellow-eyed (hoiho, *Megadyptes antipodes*), Fiordland crested (tawaki, *Eudyptes pachyrhynchus*) and little blue (kororā, *Eudyptula minor*). Yellow-eyed and Fiordland crested are the rarest of the world's 18 species, and both depend on coastal forest for breeding. Yellow-eyed colonies occur at a number of sites around the main island and on smaller islands on the east coast; Fiordland cresteds nest mainly on the Ernest Islands at the south end of Mason Bay.

Of the flying sea birds, tītī is among the commonest. Dark, darting, energetic birds, these sooty shearwaters (*Puffineus griseus*) migrate from North Pacific wintering grounds in the southern spring, when, in their millions, they return to colonies on Rakiura's Tītī Islands and the subantarctic Snares group of islands. They are daytime feeders, often in huge flocks, returning to their burrows on small islands and

TOP: Yellow-eyed penguins breed at several sites around the Stewart Island coast. MIDDLE: Sooty shearwaters by the millions feed in the waters around Stewart Island. MIKE TAYLOR BOTTOM: Buller's albatrosses are the commonest species of albatross seen off Halfmoon and Horseshoe bays.

headlands just after dark. They produce a single chick over summer and depart for the North Pacific through March–April.

The albatross family is well represented off the Rakiura coast, with Buller's mollymawk (*Thalassarche bulleri*) the mostly commonly encountered. Black-browed (*T. melanophris*) and white-capped mollymawks (*T. cauta*), and the giant northern royal albatross (*Diomedea sanfordi*) are also reasonably common along coastal waters.

Five coromorant or shag species breed at Rakiura. These include the large Foveaux shag (*Leucocarbo stewarti*), which is restricted in its breeding range to Stewart Island, adjacent islands and the South Island east coast as far as North Otago.

Of the marine mammals, the New Zealand fur seal (*Arctocephalus forsteri*) is the commonest, and there are several breeding colonies. The larger New Zealand sea lion (*Phocarctos hookeri*), the rarest of the world's sea lions and a threatened species, is also found along the coast, and in 2017 a breeding colony of sea lions was confirmed in the Port Pegasus area. Leopard seals and elephant seals on solitary migrations away from their subantarctic lair occasionally haul out on Rakiura beaches.

INTRODUCED PROBLEMS

Introduced wild animals pose the main threat to native fauna on Rakiura. Wild cats and three rat species – Norway rat, ship or black rat, and the kiore or Pacific rat – prey on birds, lizards and insects. Kiore arrived with early Māori. The large Norway rat probably came with sealers. The ship rat, more devastating on birds because it is a good climber, arrived later.

In 1964 a plague of ship rats on Big South Cape Island prompted an emergency rescue operation. Wildlife Service staff worked desperately to save the last-known South Island saddleback, snipe and bush wren populations by transferring them to predator-free islands in the vicinity. Only the saddlebacks survived, but from that operation, wildlife staff developed an expertise in island transfers of endangered species that made New Zealand a world leader in invasive-species control.

The kiore, introduced centuries ago, has cultural value to Rakiura Māori. It is the smallest of the three rat species at about half the size of the ship rat, and can climb trees and swim. It feeds on a wide range of plants and insects and, to a lesser extent, will prey on birds, lizards and bats.

Rakiura's population of white-tailed deer – the only herd of this species established in New Zealand apart from small numbers in Otago's Dart valley area – is a threat to the integrity of the forest, although recreational hunting is helping to keep numbers in check. Introduced from the United States in 1905, they are widely distributed on the main island, and have seriously depleted some coastal areas of forest in the past. Red deer also occur on the main island, having been introduced into the Freshwater valley in 1901, but their numbers are lower and they are found mostly in central or northwest areas of the island.

Equally concerning to wildlife managers is the possum (the Australian brush-tailed possum, *Trichosurus vulpecula*), liberated in 1890 for its potential contribution to the fur trade. Through overbrowsing, possums can kill canopy trees such as rātā, kamahi (*Weinmannia racemosa*) and tōtara. It was

The Australian brush-tailed possum is a serious threat to Stewart Island ecology. DEPARTMENT OF CONSERVATION

recently discovered that possums may also take eggs from the nests of burrowing or tree-nesting birds.

Much of the Department of Conservation's species-protection work on the island is about predator control. A wild-cat control programme to protect the last remaining mainland population of kākāpō, carried out in the Pegasus area in the 1970s, turned into a rescue mission when it became apparent that kākāpō were losing the battle against the cats. An alarming number of radio-tagged kākāpō turned up dead – killed by cats – which led to the decision to transfer the remaining birds to island sanctuaries. The protection of nesting southern New Zealand dotterels from predation by wild cats is an ongoing focus for the Department of Conservation. After five years' cat-control work – beginning on Table Hill in 1994 – the dotterel population more than doubled.

Of major significance for wildlife protection on Rakiura is the absence of stoats, ferrets and weasels, mustelids that are widely distributed through the North and South islands, where they cause untold destruction to vulnerable wildlife. Rakiura's natural environment has also benefited from the absence of feral pigs, goats, rabbits and hares. Surprisingly, mice do not occur on the island either. Being free of these introduced animals has helped Rakiura retain much of its rare and special character.

Among invasive plants introduced into Rakiura, the Department of Conservation is concerned about the spread of marram grass and tree lupin on dunes, and of gorse, Darwin's barberry and the invasive clematis, old man's beard, along various parts of the coastline.

5

POINTS SOUTH

SOUTH OF TABLE HILL, the landscape of Rakiura acquires qualities that are alluring and bleakly beautiful – granite domes, stunted forest, forbidding shores, exposed wave-battered headlands, and numerous islands and islets – a landscape wind-worried and hunkered down. In the south, Rakiura National Park offers new dimensions in land forms and life forms. It is a wild place with a whiff of the subantarctic about it. Only 100 km to the southwest lies The Snares group of islands and the subantarctic proper.

The main island tapers to points marked by South Cape/Whiore and nearby South West Cape/Puhiwaero. At this remote location foundered the hopes for 'Terra Australis Incognita', the great unknown southern continent postulated down the centuries by Greek and other European philosophers.

The landmarks of the south are the Tin Range, Port Pegasus/Pikihatiti, the Fraser Peaks, South Cape and the Tītī/Muttonbird Islands off to the west. Dotted about the landscape east and west of the Tin Range are

The bare granite peak of Gog (407 m) dominates the skyline in the Pegasus area. LOU SANSON

Nature's crucibles: water-filled holes in the bare granite of Magog in the Pegasus area. Gog is in the distance. LOU SANSON

the extraordinary domes and cones of bare silver-grey granite that project a 'lost world' atmosphere. Most striking of all are the peaks of Gog and Magog west of Port Pegasus, which caused a stir among James Cook's 1770 expedition as *Endeavour* sailed towards South Cape and saw the peaks bathed in morning sunlight. Cook thought the rock some kind of marble. His scientific leader, Joseph Banks, said the mineral 'shone as if it had been polishd or rather lookd as if they were realy pavd with glass'. First mate Richard Pickersgill wrote of the domes as 'remarkable Peaks resembling sugar loaves'. Their names, drawn from mythology, are appropriate given their haunting appearance, especially in mist and drizzle.

Responding to the cooler, damper, cloudier conditions, the vegetation here is different to that found in the northeast of the island. Tall forest is confined largely to the coastal fringes; above that rimu and rātā are stunted, and the main podocarp species is yellow-silver pine. Upland rātā trees are often found growing horizontally, a response to exposure to high winds. Prominent in the shrubland are the hardy leatherwood, mānuka and inaka, the grass tree. Snow tussocks include endemic species.

In recognition of the special nature of southern Rakiura, the bulk of it was declared a nature reserve before the creation of the national park. The reserve sprawled across 67,400 ha – 40 per cent of the total land area. Strictly speaking, trampers needed permits to visit the Tin Range

OPPOSITE, TOP: South Arm, Port Pegasus. LOU SANSON OPPOSITE, BOTTOM: Granite islands in the cool clear water of Cook Arm, Port Pegasus. Magog is in the distance.

and other areas in the south but in practice they were not required to have them. Few people ever ventured here and few do these days, so human impacts are minimal.

The sheltered waters and land of Port Pegasus, in the lee of westerly winds, have made it welcoming for mariners through the ages. Named after an 1809 sealing vessel, Port Pegasus has three islands (with four navigable entrances adjacent to them) guarding its inner bays and channels. It is a haven for fishing vessels working southern fishing grounds, and an adventurous destination for yachties, divers, recreational anglers and trampers.

Pegasus has a notable place in Stewart Island history – it's where British sovereignty was claimed over 'Stewart's Island' on 5 June 1840. When HMS *Herald* came south collecting signatures from Māori chiefs for the Treaty of Waitangi, instead of calling first at Rakiura's small northern settlements it made landfall at Pegasus, which was then deserted. The colours of Her Majesty Queen Victoria were hoisted, and the declaration of sovereignty was buried in a bottle on a small tidal island in the harbour.

Port Pegasus in the 19th-century heyday of tin mining and commercial fishing had a settlement with a hotel and post office. RAKIURA MUSEUM

Historical names and dates carved into a rock wall in Port Pegasus and dating from the 1800s.

Earlier, in 1826, a small party of colonists led by English shipbuilder William Cook settled at Port Pegasus. They were tough but their shipbuilding industry did not survive. Commercial fishing and tin mining brought people back to Pegasus. The mining lasted just two years, 1888–90, and the Pegasus fish processing ended when Halfmoon Bay became the industry's main base in the 1920s.

Apart from teams of wildlife staff working on wild-cat control and kākāpō recovery in the 1970s and 1980s, Pegasus has remained uninhabited. Its many coves offer endless hours of exploring, and Gog and Magog are destinations for occasional day trampers. Many of them walk via the gently shelving 3 km-long Cook Arm, where the tide laps in and out gradually, providing a walkway at low tide almost its whole length. Its southern bank allows easy walking too, across expanses of matted wire rush and other low vegetation.

The southwest coast of the main island has no inhabitants and is little visited. There are no inlets, and safe harbours are few and far between. In contrast, the southwest Tītī Islands – with Taukihepa/Big South Cape Island the largest – are visited at regular intervals by Māori muttonbird parties and teams of conservation staff working with endangered species.

MUTTONBIRDING

The seasonal harvest of muttonbirds was a primary reason for Māori occupation of Rakiura. It has been a practice for centuries and continues today. The term muttonbird applies to the young tītī or sooty shearwater, whose flesh was likened to sheep meat.

When the adult birds stop feeding their chick about the beginning of April, the harvest begins. At first the young birds are pulled from their burrows and quickly killed, but later in the season, when they are venturing from their burrows at night, the hunting is done by torchlight.

In pre-European times torches were made from tōtara bark lashed with flax fronds and soaked in muttonbird fat. The harvested tītī were cooked and packed in their own fat in pouches (pōhā) made of bull kelp. Salt is the preserving agent today.

Muttonbirding was specified in the 1864 Deed of Cession between Rakiura Māori and the government as an inalienable right of Rakiura Māori and their descendants. There are 21 birding islands in all, in two main groups – off the southwest and northeast (Foveaux) coasts of the main island. Between seasons the muttonbirding camps are usually deserted.

Harvested muttonbirds – an acquired taste – are distributed among family members or sold to outlets in the towns and cities. Connoisseurs across the country eagerly look forward to their arrival some time in April. In recent years Māori have commissioned research into the impact of harvesting at the tītī colonies and the issue of sustainable yield.

Mecca for muttonbirders – Taukihepa/Big South Cape Island. Putauhinu is the largest of the distant islands.

FURTHER READING

Brown, Rob, 2006, *Rakiura: The wilderness of Stewart Island*, Nelson, Craig Potton Publishing

Goodwillie, Ulva, 2010, *Ulva Island: A visitor's guide,* Invercargill, Craigs Design and Print

Hall-Jones, John, 1994, *Stewart Island Explored*, Invercargill, Craig Printing

Peat, Neville, 2010, *Rakiura Heritage: A Stewart Island history and guide to historic sites*, Invercargill, Department of Conservation

Watt, J.P.C., 2014. *The Whalers' Base: Facts, photos and people associated with the Norwegian presence in Paterson Inlet, Stewart Island, New Zealand, 1924–36*, Havelock North, published by the author

INDEX